# WATER ENERGY

**GRAHAM RICKARD**

Garthamlock Secondary School

43 Craigievar Street

GLASGOW G33 5HG

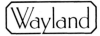

Titles in the series

W/D

**Bioenergy**
**Geothermal Energy**
**Solar Energy**
**Water Energy**
**Wind Energy**

***Cover:*** *The Hondo Dam on the Rio Dulce, Argentina. Hydroelectric power now constitutes about 6.7 per cent of the world's supply of electricity.*

***Series Editor:*** *William Wharfe*

***Designer:*** *Charles Harford HSD*

First published in 1990 by
Wayland (Publishers) Limited
61 Western Road, Hove
East Sussex BN3 1JD, England

© Copyright 1990 Wayland (Publishers) Limited

**British Library Cataloguing and Publication Data**
Rickard, Graham
  Water energy
  1. Water power
  I. Title II. Series
  621.20422

ISBN 1 85210 905 X

Phototypeset by Rachel Gibbs, Wayland
Printed in Italy by G. Canale & C.S.p.A, Turin
Bound in Belgium by Casterman S.A.

Words that are in the glossary are printed in **bold** type the first time they appear in the text.

# Contents

# WHY ALTERNATIVE ENERGY?

Energy is the ability to do work. Energy is all around us. All animals and plants need energy in order to live. All machines need concentrated supplies of energy to make them work. As the world's population increases and people use more machines, more energy is needed to drive them. The world's demand for energy has increased more than ten times since the beginning of this century.

Most of this energy is in the form of electricity. This is usually produced by burning the three main 'fossil fuels' – coal, oil and gas – to boil water, to produce the steam that powers **turbines** to **generate** electricity. Every hour, more than 500,000 tonnes of fossil fuels are burnt around the world. These supplies are not replaceable, and new sources of energy will have to be found before fossil fuels run out.

*Fossil fuels cause pollution.* **Left** *Oil pollution in the sea being cleared up.* **Right** *Coal-fired power stations caused the acid rain that killed these trees.*

**Above** *Coal-fired power stations release large amounts of pollution into the atmosphere. This causes acid rain, which kills trees and pollutes lakes. Here we see the chimneys of a coal-fired power station in Romania.*

There is enough oil and gas in the world for about fifty years, while coal will last longer – about 300 years. These fuels cause serious damage to the **environment.** When they burn, they produce poisonous gases which fall as 'acid rain'. This pollutes vast areas of lakes and forests, killing fish and trees. Some of these gases also contribute to the '**greenhouse effect**' which is gradually warming up the Earth's atmosphere. So people all over the world are looking for sources of 'alternative energy'. By this they mean an alternative to using fossil fuels.

Some people see the use of nuclear power as a clean and safe alternative to fossil fuels, but this produces highly dangerous waste products. Also, nuclear energy depends on supplies of uranium, which are expected to run out in the next sixty years.

This book looks at the many different ways of using water energy. The energy in water is a renewable energy source. Unlike coal or oil it will not run out. If we can find efficient ways of using that energy we will have a power supply for the future that is safe, cheap and clean.

# THE POWER OF WATER

Four-fifths of the world is covered by water. The water in our oceans and rivers is constantly on the move. Waves, currents, tides, flowing rivers and waterfalls all contain vast amounts of **kinetic** (movement) energy. This could be used as a convenient source of energy by converting it into electricity. Increased use of water energy could reduce our need to use traditional energy sources, such as fossil fuels.

The movement of water is one of our oldest energy sources. The water-wheel was probably first used in Greece, in the first century BC. By the Middle Ages, water-wheels were used throughout Europe and Asia: for grinding corn, powering bellows

**Below** *The view from space shows just how much of the Earth's surface is covered by water. Here we see both the Pacific Ocean (**left**) and the Atlantic Ocean (**right**).*

and hammers in iron forges and **irrigating** fields. Tidal mills (see page 10) on river **estuaries** were also used in similar ways.

**Above** *The water in the Niagara Falls (on the border between Canada and the USA) drops 47 m and contains huge amounts of kinetic energy.*

**Right** *A river provides the power for this old mill in Virginia, USA. The mill is used for grinding corn.*

**Above** *This industrial water-wheel powers a hammer for shaping metal.*

The water-wheel was the original power source of the **Industrial Revolution**, driving the machinery of the first factories. These factories were usually built alongside rivers, to make sure there would be a constant source of power. Eventually, the invention of steam engines that could drive bigger machines than water-wheels, meant that water-wheels were no longer used. In the UK, there are 20,000 sites where water-wheels were once used. Today, almost all this water power is running to waste.

**Hydroelectric** power (HEP) schemes have so far proved the most successful way of harnessing water energy. Moving water, from rivers or reservoirs, is used to turn the turbines that drive **generators** to produce electricity.

The seas and oceans are also possible good energy sources. Some schemes already in use depend on the rise and fall of the tides to generate electricity. Some experiments have tried to capture the power of the waves, but so far this is proving much more difficult and costly than other forms of water energy.

Although generating electricity from water energy produces little pollution, the use of any form of energy has its drawbacks. Building hydroelectric dams, for example, often means flooding vast areas of land. In the same way **barrages** (barriers) used in tidal power stations could change the natural **habitat** of many plants, animals and birds along the sea shore.

The following chapters look at the different ways in which people have used water energy and how it may be used in future.

**Above** *The Gordon Dam in Tasmania. Dams like this collect huge amounts of water, which can be used as part of hydroelectric schemes (see page 21).*

# ENERGY FROM THE TIDES

Every day, the gravity of both the Sun and Moon pulls on the Earth and causes vast quantities of water to move around the world's seas. We call these movements tides.

Tidal power was first harnessed by tidal mills (water-wheels powered by tidal waters) around 1,000 years ago. At high tide, water was trapped behind a floodgate, and then released to drive a water-wheel as the tide was going out. Modern tidal power stations work in a similar way. They capture the water behind a barrage (a large wall) at high tide. At low tide the water is released through turbines to produce electricity.

**Below** *The gravity of the Sun and Moon causes the tides.*

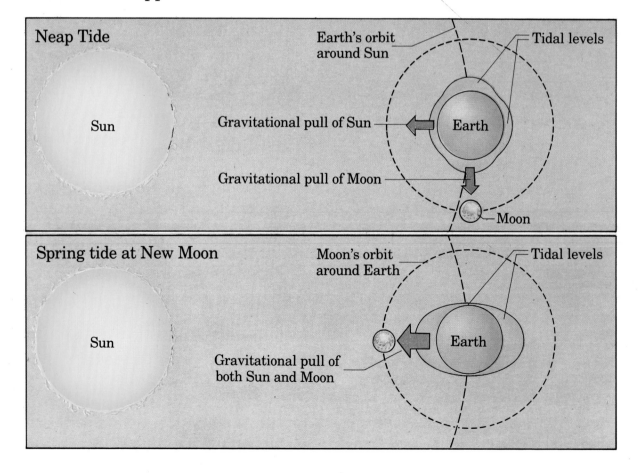

**Above** *The barrage over the River Rance, seen as the tide goes out.*

Tidal schemes are already in use in France, the USSR, China and Canada. The best-known project is on the estuary of the River Rance, near St Malo in northern France. The tide here rises and falls 13.5 m. The power station consists of a single barrage across the estuary. This contains 24 turbines that produce 320 **megawatts (MW)** of electricity – enough to boil about 150,000 kettles. The barrage is a long straight dam with a road on top, so that it acts as a bridge as well as a power station. The turbines work in two directions: both as the water flows into the estuary as the tide comes in, and as the tide goes out.

Tidal power schemes work best where there is a large estuary and a large tidal range (a big difference between sea level at high tide and low tide). A possible site for a large tidal barrage is the Bay of Fundy, in Canada. The scheme that is proposed would

**Above** *An artist's impression of the future Severn barrage.*

generate the same amount of electricity as a conventional power station (coal, oil or nuclear), at about the same cost.

Several sites around the UK are ideally suited to use tidal energy. Tidal barrages could produce as much as 8 per cent of the UK's energy needs. One of the best sites is the Severn estuary which has one of the largest tidal ranges in the world – 11 m. The proposed Severn Barrage would be 18 km long and would contain 216 turbines, with **sluices** to control the flow of water on either side. Enormous **locks** at one end would allow shipping to pass the barrage. The amount of electricity produced would be about 8,000 MW.

Tidal barrages, like HEP stations, are expensive and difficult to build (see page 23). However, when completed, they produce cheap electricity, use no fuel and are easy to run and maintain. But one major problem with tidal power stations is that they do not always produce power when it is most needed. This is because the times of high and low tide are constantly changing.

Tidal power stations have their own environmental problems. Migrating fish, such as salmon and eels, use estuaries and rivers for breeding. They might be affected by passing through turbines. Estuaries and tidal mud-flats are important habitats for many forms of wildlife. A barrage can change both the amount of salt in the water and the length of time that the mud-flats are under water.

Some people fear that these changes might harm the wildlife in the area. However, a tidal barrage scheme creates a large basin of calm water. This could encourage the growth of tourism and water sports.

**Opposite** *How a tidal barrage works.*

## Tidal Barrage

A. At high tide the sluice gates are opened. The water turns the turbines on its way to the basin behind the barrage.

B. At low tide the water is let out from the basin to the sea. This is when the greatest amount of electricity can be produced.

1. Basin (water held back behind barrage)
2. Barrage
3. Turbine
4. Sluice gates
5. Generator
6. Control room

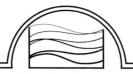

# POWER FROM WAVES

Every day, the world's coasts are battered by waves of enormous power. Ocean waves are created by winds blowing over the sea. Scientists have been looking for ways of turning the constant rising and falling of waves into useful energy.

In some places, waves can be up to 25 m high. It is estimated that the energy in one metre's length of the biggest waves along some coasts could generate 100 **kilowatts (kW)** of power. Even if only a third of this can be converted into electricity, wave power stations could become possible in the future.

Over 300 designs for wave-energy converters already exist. In some designs, the up-and-down movement of a device floating in the water is used to pump **fluid** to turbines that drive a generator. The Salter's Duck design consists of twenty to thirty 'ducks' or floats. The bobbing motion of the ducks drives a pump. The pump turns a turbine, which drives a generator. The Salter's Duck uses most of the waves' energy.

One of the most successful designs uses the **Oscillating** Water Column (OWC) principle. A box with an underwater opening contains a column of water, which acts like a piston in a cylinder. As the water column moves up and down with the waves, air is forced in and out through a turbine at the top. This drives a generator.

**Below** *Waves contain large amounts of kinetic energy.*

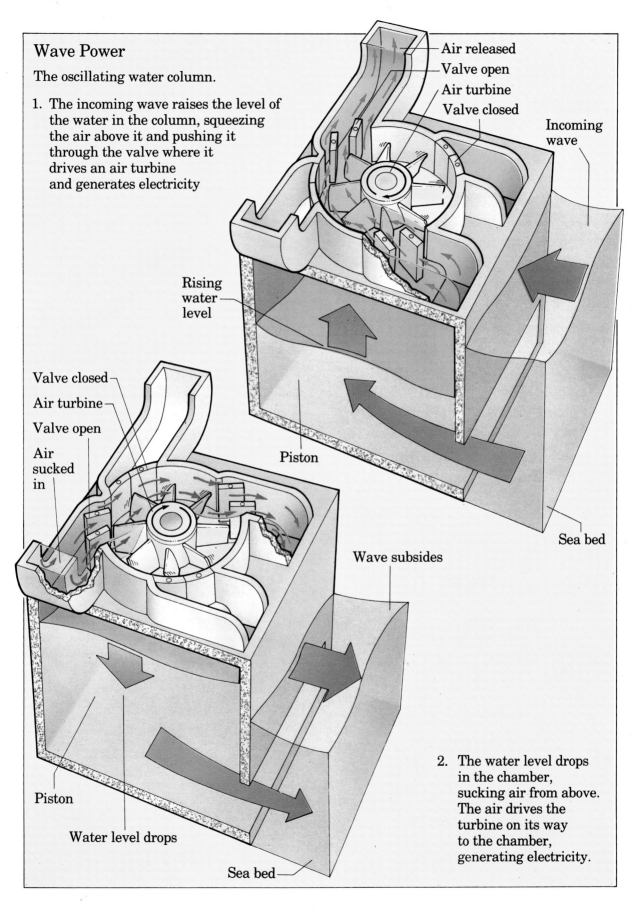

# Wave Power

The oscillating water column.

1. The incoming wave raises the level of the water in the column, squeezing the air above it and pushing it through the valve where it drives an air turbine and generates electricity

Air released

Valve open

Air turbine

Valve closed

Incoming wave

Rising water level

Sea bed

Piston

Valve closed

Air turbine

Valve open

Air sucked in

Piston

Water level drops

Wave subsides

Sea bed

2. The water level drops in the chamber, sucking air from above. The air drives the turbine on its way to the chamber, generating electricity.

The first successful OWC device was used in Japan to power a light on a navigation **buoy**. An OWC device has been installed on a cliff at Tofteshallen in Norway. It is one of the most advanced wave-energy devices in the world, and can generate 500 kW of power.

Wave energy devices are difficult to build, because they must be strong enough to withstand battering from wind and waves, and some designs have to be light enough to float. It is also important to be able to store some of the electricity produced when the sea is rough, so that power can be provided even when the sea is calm. It is possible that a pumped-water storage system like that at Dinorwic (see page 24) could be used to store the waves' energy.

Wave-energy power stations would be expensive to build, difficult to anchor and might pose a danger to shipping. They would also interfere with the wave pattern on nearby shores.

**Below** *This is an artist's impression of a large-scale wave power scheme, with rows of wave power machines.*

This might affect beaches and wildlife. However, scientists hope to develop small wave-energy devices. These would be useful in providing power for small, isolated coastal communities, which now depend on expensive diesel fuel to generate electricity.

**Right** *The wave power machine built on the cliffs at Tofteshallen in Norway. In 1989 this wave power machine was itself damaged during a fierce storm. Future devices will have to be stronger.*

**Below** *Wave power machines must be designed to stand up to the destructive force of storms at sea.*

# HEAT FROM THE SEA

In hot climates, the sea stores vast amounts of the Sun's heat. This can be converted into electricity. The idea of using heat from the sea was first thought of over 100 years ago. However, it was not until the 1920s that the first electricity generating process was devised. The process is called Ocean Thermal Energy Conversion (OTEC).

In tropical regions, the upper, Sun-heated seawater is much warmer than the deeper water. At the Equator, for example, the temperature changes from 26 °C at the surface to about 4.5 °C at a depth of 750 m. The OTEC unit uses warm water from the upper layer to evaporate a liquid that boils at a very low temperature, such as ammonia or freon. The gas produced by the evaporation is used in the same way as is steam in a conventional power station.

**Opposite** *A possible OTEC design put forward by Lockheed.*

**Below** *In tropical regions the Sun heats the sea, and this warmth can be used to produce electricity.*

1. Equipment handling area
2. Crew living quarters
3. Warm surface water (26°C) inlet
4. Ammonia storage
5. Ballast tanks
6. Evaporator
7. Turbines
8. Control room
9. Generator
10. Condenser
11. Buoyancy tanks
12. Cold water inlet (4.5°C) from about 750m depth
13. Cables transmitting electricity to mainland
14. Cold water outlet
15. Warm water outlet

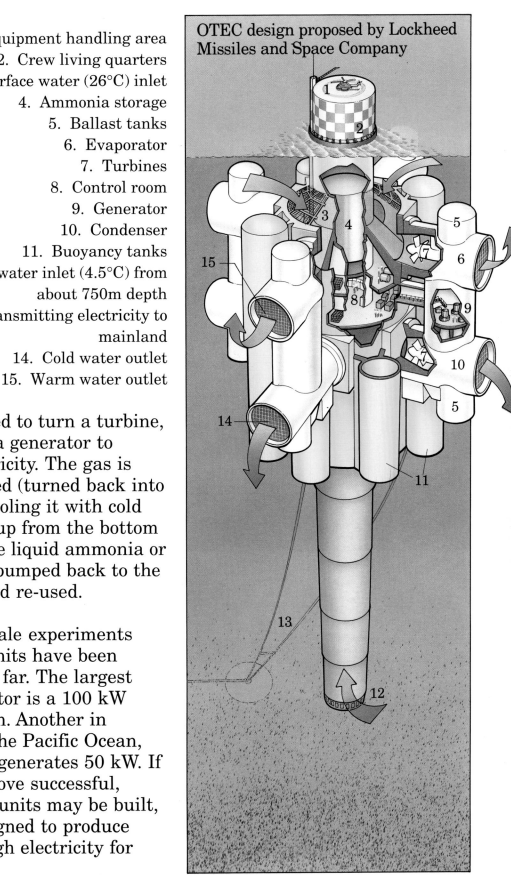

OTEC design proposed by Lockheed Missiles and Space Company

The gas is used to turn a turbine, which drives a generator to produce electricity. The gas is then condensed (turned back into a liquid) by cooling it with cold water drawn up from the bottom of the sea. The liquid ammonia or freon is then pumped back to the evaporator and re-used.

Only small-scale experiments with OTEC units have been carried out so far. The largest OTEC generator is a 100 kW plant in Japan. Another in operation in the Pacific Ocean, near Hawaii, generates 50 kW. If these tests prove successful, bigger OTEC units may be built, probably designed to produce 2 MW – enough electricity for 1,000 homes.

**Below** *This diagram shows a typical HEP scheme.*

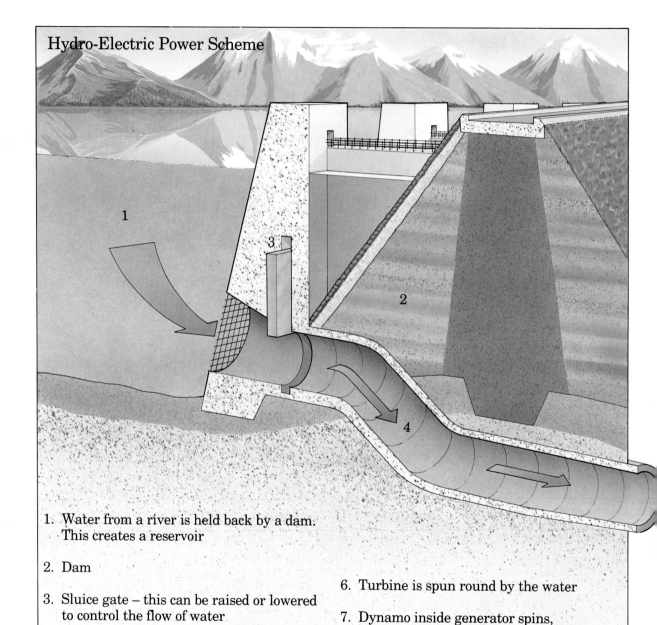

**Hydro-Electric Power Scheme**

1. Water from a river is held back by a dam. This creates a reservoir

2. Dam

3. Sluice gate – this can be raised or lowered to control the flow of water

4. Water flows down through tunnel, gathering speed

5. Tunnel gets narrower – this increases the speed of the water through the turbine

6. Turbine is spun round by the water

7. Dynamo inside generator spins, generating electricity

8. Control room

9. Water flows out of the turbine back to the river

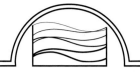

# HYDROELECTRIC POWER

Falling water is probably the world's largest renewable energy source. The Sun evaporates water from the Earth's surface. The water then falls as rain, snow and hail over hills and mountains and flows back down to the sea. HEP uses the kinetic energy of falling water, either in a natural river or from a reservoir created by an artificial dam. This water is fed through channels to turn turbines, which drive electrical generators.

The amount of electricity that these generators can produce depends on how much water is flowing, and how far the water has fallen before it goes through the turbines.

**Below** *The power station where the electricity is produced.*

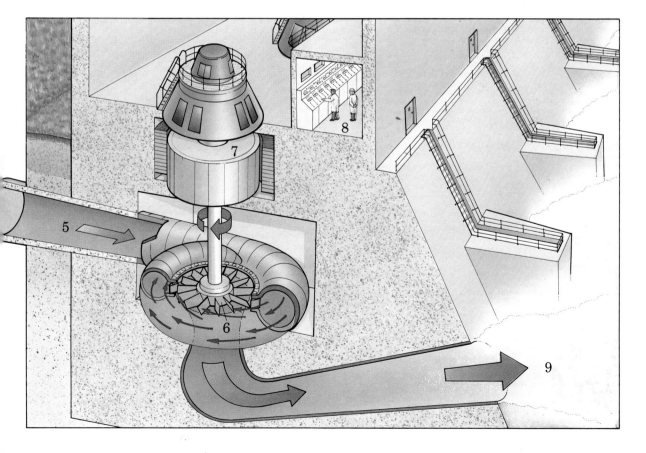

**Above** *The Grand Coulee dam, the largest HEP scheme in the USA.*

**Above** *You can see the tops of generators in this HEP station.*

A small amount of water falling from a great height can produce as much power as a large amount of water falling a shorter distance. By damming a river high up in a mountain and piping the water to turbines much further down, a constant and powerful supply of electricity can be produced.

In some ways, HEP is a cheap source of power. However, it is expensive to build a dam, power station and **transmission lines**.

For instance, imagine the expense of building a concrete dam 170m tall! Yet that is the size of the dam in the Grand Coulee HEP scheme in Washington State, USA. It supplies electricity to thousands of people in northwestern USA.

Once the HEP scheme is in place the cost of producing electricity is small. Water is free, and a large HEP station can be run by only a few people. No fuel is needed, and the same river can be dammed at several different places as it flows downhill, using the same water to produce even more power. However, some of the world's countries cannot afford to use their rivers for HEP because of the initial building costs. The UK, USA, USSR and China have all helped to build HEP schemes in developing countries.

HEP can also cause environmental problems. Huge dams built to raise the water level flood enormous areas of land. Whenever water is diverted from one area to another, it can have a serious effect on the plants and wildlife that live in both areas. It can also have useful effects. For instance, in Australia, irrigation from HEP schemes has helped to turn previously dry, semi-desert regions into rich, green farmland.

HEP can also be used to store energy. In the early hours of the day, when people are asleep, there is a very low demand for electricity. However, the conventional power stations cannot just 'switch off', so there is a lot of electricity available at this time, which frequently goes to waste.

**Below** *HEP can provide water to irrigate farmland that would otherwise be dry.*

**Above** *Inside the 'Electric Mountain' at Dinorwic in North Wales.*

**Above** *A small-scale hydroelectric turbine.*

In a pumped-water storage system, this surplus electricity is used to pump up water into a large reservoir. When an extra supply of electricity is needed, the water is allowed to fall to a lower reservoir, powering turbines as it falls.

This type of system was built at Dinorwic, in North Wales. It is called the 'Electric Mountain' because the water falls through tunnels hollowed out of a mountain on its way from the higher reservoir to the lower one. Dinorwic produces enough electricity to light up a city.

Large-scale HEP schemes already produce 6.7 per cent of the world's total energy need – twice as much as the nuclear industry's share.

There is now evidence that small-scale HEP schemes could be very useful for small or remote communities. They would provide cheap electricity for communities that presently rely on generators powered by expensive diesel fuel. Scientists have improved designs of small-scale turbines and generators so much that they can now operate even in fairly shallow rivers.

## THE SNOWY POWERHOUSE

One of the best examples of large-scale hydroelectric power in action is the Snowy Mountains scheme in Australia.
Australia is the driest and flattest of all the continents. Half the land receives less than 300 mm of rain a year, and most of the rest of the country receives less than 600 mm. Australia's largest river is the Murray. It takes a whole year to empty into the sea as much water as South America's largest river, the Amazon, discharges in one-and-a-half days. The only area in Australia that is 'wet' is the Great Dividing Range of mountains.

The Great Dividing Range stretches from north to south along the eastern edge of the country. Winds from the sea drop their moisture as they cross these mountains. This rain and snow forms hundreds of streams and rivers. Near the border of New South Wales and Victoria, the mountain range rises to about 2,100 m above sea level and is

**Below** *The Snowy Mountains HEP Scheme being built in the 1950s.*

known here as the Snowy Mountains. The three main rivers in the area are the Snowy River, with its tributary the Eucumbene, the Murray and the Murrumbidgee.

After the Second World War, Australia needed to produce more energy to supply its rapid growth in industry. Also, more water was needed for growing the crops. Several ideas were put forward to use the waters of the Snowy River for electrical power and for irrigation. In 1949, the Snowy Mountains Hydroelectric Authority was set up to undertake the huge project, which took twenty-five years to complete.

The Snowy Mountains Scheme diverts the waters of the Snowy River and the Eucumbene through two massive systems of tunnels. These feed the Murray and Murrumbidgee with extra water for irrigation. The water falls 790 m through shafts, tunnels and power stations to generate electricity.

The 'Snowy' is the largest hydroelectric scheme in the world, covering an area of over 3,200 km² and it cost almost

£450 million to build. It includes 16 large dams, 7 power stations, over 145 km of tunnels, 80 km of **aqueducts,** a pumping station, and hundreds of kilometres of transmission lines. It is one of the largest engineering projects in Australia. It provides 3,740 MW of electricity and huge quantities of water for irrigation.

**Opposite** *This diagram shows one section of the huge Snowy scheme.*

**Below** *Water drops 450 m through pipes to the Murray I station.*

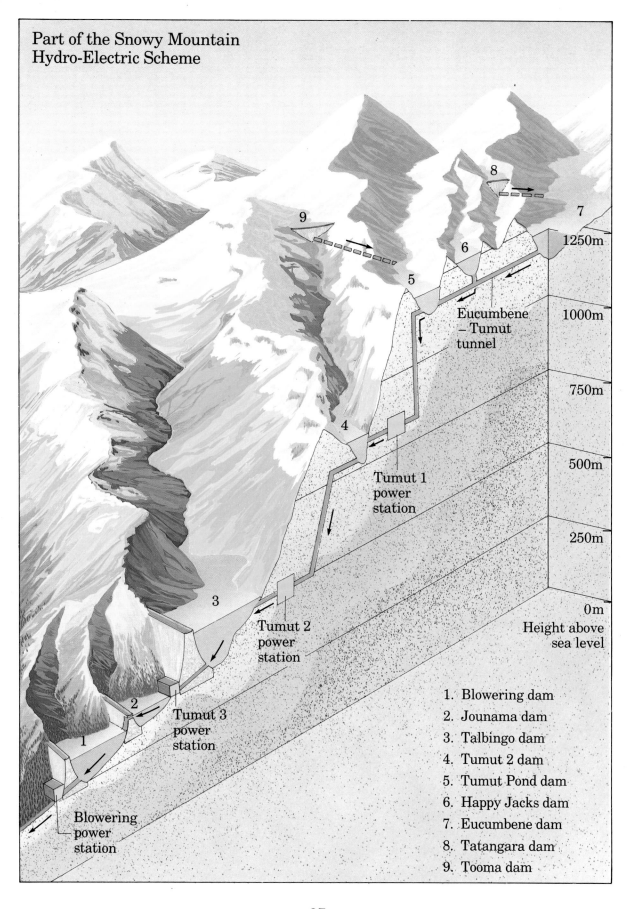

Part of the Snowy Mountain
Hydro-Electric Scheme

8

9

7

1250m

Eucumbene
– Tumut
tunnel

1000m

750m

5

4

Tumut 1
power
station

500m

250m

3

Tumut 2
power
station

0m

Height above
sea level

2

Tumut 3
power
station

1

Blowering
power
station

1. Blowering dam
2. Jounama dam
3. Talbingo dam
4. Tumut 2 dam
5. Tumut Pond dam
6. Happy Jacks dam
7. Eucumbene dam
8. Tatangara dam
9. Tooma dam

6

# PROJECT

## You will need:

- A 4.5 volt electric motor (or, better, a small dynamo)
- A 1.5 volt light bulb
- Stiff plastic (eg plastic drinks bottle)
- A cork
- Two washing-up bottle tops
- Electric wires
- A coat hanger
- A large gear
- A small gear
- Glue (non-water soluble)
- Wooden boards (see diagram)
- The casing of a used ball-point pen

## To make a small hydroelectric device:

1 Ask an adult to cut the bottom off a wire coat hanger and to push it lengthways through the cork so that about 1 cm is pushed right through.

2 Cut eight strips of stiff plastic (from a used washing up liquid bottle) of the same length as the cork, and about 3.5 cm wide.

3 Ask an adult to cut grooves lengthways into the cork, so that you can slot the plastic strips into it (see diagram).

4 Glue the plastic strips into the grooves in the cork. They should stick out at least 3 cm.

5 Slide the other end of the coat hanger (the spindle) through the pen case and washing-up bottle tops (see diagram) and fix the large gear on the end of it.

6 Place the spindle and cork on a sink so that the cork is under the cold tap.

7 Tape the pen case to a piece of board, and tape the board to the draining board.

8 Fix the motor to a piece of board and push the small gear on to the motor's spindle. Connect the motor to the light bulb with the wires.

9 Turn on the tap so that the water-wheel spins. Holding the board on which the motor is mounted, press the motor's small gear against the spinning large gear.

## What should happen:

As the motor's spindle turns, the motor acts as a generator, producing a current of electricity that makes the bulb glow. What happens as the water-wheel spins faster or slower?

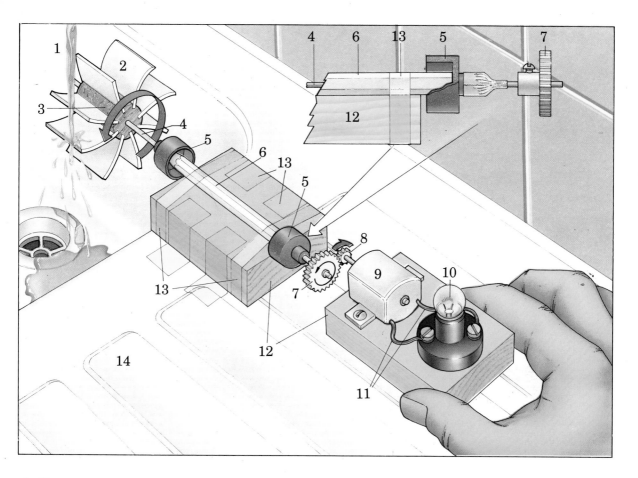

1. Tap water
2. Strips cut from plastic drinks bottle
3. Cork
4. Wire from coat hanger
5. Washing-up bottle top
6. Casing of a used ball-point pen
7. Large gear
8. Small gear
9. 4.5v motor
10. 1.5v light bulb
11. Electric wires
12. Wooden blocks
13. Sticky tape
14. Draining board

**Above** *Press the gears together firmly so that the motor's spindle turns around quickly. The faster the spindle turns, the more electricity you will generate.*

## Note:

The water-wheel will spray water in all directions. Make sure that nothing that can be damaged by water is in range. Wear water-proof clothing. You can reduce the amount of spray by placing a large see-through plastic bag over the tap and water-wheel – though make sure the bag does not become tangled in the wheel!

# GLOSSARY

**Aqueduct:** A man-made channel for carrying water above the ground.

**Barrage:** A large barrier across an estuary, built to hold back water.

**Buoy:** A float that is anchored at sea as a guide to shipping.

**Environment:** The things that make up a place, for example the weather, the water and the plants.

**Estuary:** The mouth of a river.

**Fluid:** A liquid or gas.

**Generate:** To produce.

**Generator:** A machine that produces electricity.

**Greenhouse effect:** As some gases – like carbon dioxide – build up in the atmosphere, they prevent the Sun's heat from escaping. In this way they act like the glass of a greenhouse. The greenhouse effect is gradually warming up the Earth's atmosphere.

**Habitat:** The place where an animal or plant usually lives.

**Hydroelectric:** Producing electricity from falling water.

**Industrial Revolution:** The rapid development of industry, first in Britain, and then in Western Europe and the USA, during the eighteenth and nineteenth centuries.

**Irrigating:** Supplying water to dry land.

**Kilowatt (kW):** A thousand watts (see watt). A kilowatt will power a one bar electric heater.

**Kinetic energy:** The energy contained in a moving object.

**Lock:** A device for raising or lowering ships from one water level to another.

**Megawatt (MW):** A million watts (see kilowatt).

**Oscillating:** Swinging to and fro, or up and down.

**Sluice:** A gate for stopping or controlling the flow of water.

**Transmission lines:** The cables that carry electrical power.

**Turbine:** A device that has blades like a propeller, which turns to drive an electrical generator.

**Watt (W):** The unit of electrical power.

**Picture Acknowledgements**

The artwork on pages 10,13,15,19, 20, 21, 27 and 29 is by Nick Hawken.

The publishers would like to thank the following for providing the illustrations in this book: J. Allan Cash Picture Library 4 (left), 5, 6, 7 (above), 26; Bruce Coleman 8; Energy Technology Support Unit 12, 16, 24 (right); Environmental Picture Library 17 (above); Geoscience Features Picture Library 4 (right); Robert Harding Picture Library *cover*; National Power 11; Oxford Scientific Films 7 (below); Photri 18; Science Photo Library 24 (left); Snowy Mountains Hydro-Electric Authority 22 (right), 25; Tony Stone 23; Tasmanian Hydro-Electric Commission 9; Topham Picture Library 17 (below); United States Department of Energy 22 (left); Zefa Picture Library 14.

# Further reading

*Energy: A Guidebook* by Janet
Ramage (Oxford University
Press, 1983)
*Energy Without End The Case for
Renewable Energy* by Michael
Flood (Friends of the Earth,
1986)
*Fun With Science* by Brenda
Walpole (Kingfisher, 1988)
*Fun With Science — Moving* by
Brenda Walpole (Kingfisher,
1988)
*Fun With Science — Water* by
Brenda Walpole (Kingfisher,
1988)
*Future Sources of Energy* by
Mark Lambert (Wayland, 1986)
*Only One Earth. The Care and
Maintenance of a Small Planet*
by Barbara Ward and Rene
Dubos (Penguin, 1976)
*Renewable Energy, The Power to
Choose* by Daniel Doudney and
Christopher Flavin (Norton,
1983)
*The Energy Question* By Gerald
Foley (Penguin, 1976)
*Water Power* by Ed Catherall
(Wayland, 1981)

# Further information
## Australia

The Snowy Mountains Hydro-
Electric Authority
PO Box 332
Cooma
NSW 2630

## Canada

Energy, Mines and Resources
580 Booth Street
Ottawa
Ontario K1A OE4

## New Zealand

Water Resources Survey
Department of Scientific and
Industrial Research
PO Box 29.199
Christchurch

## UK

National Power
Film Library
Parkhall Road Trading Estate
Unit B11
Dulwich SE21 8EL

Renewable Energy Promotion
Group
Energy Technology Support Unit
Building 156
Harwell Laboratory
Oxfordshire OX11 ORA

The Centre For Alternative
Technology
Machynlleth
Powys
Wales SY20 9AZ

# INDEX

Page numbers in **bold** refer to illustrations.